CW01081017

Kings
and
Queens

OF ENGLAND AND GREAT BRITAIN

by

Anne & Paul Fryer

THIS BOOK BELONGS TO

The Blows
Family

ISBN: 978-1-716-43620-8

Written by Anne Fryer

Designed and Illiustrated by Paul Fryer

For Henry and Archie

Introduction

This pocketbook has been written as a very brief introduction to the Kings and Queens of England and Great Britain.

The aim is to give the reader a basic account of the main events of each reign developing a chronological story of our Monarchy - a very British institution!

Do not expect a sophisticated evaluation of each Monarch, or detailed accounts of parliaments, wars, marriages and other events in each reign.

But I do hope you learn some interesting facts, and a desire to find out more! The illustrations by themselves tell a lot about each Monarch and have all been lovingly hand-drawn by Paul.

Anne Fryer, Author
November 2020

Æthelstan

924 - 927 King of the Anglo-Saxons
927 - 939 King of the English

Famed for being the first King of the area called England that we know today. He was the grandson of Alfred the Great.

During the 10th Century the Danes occupied part of England. Athelstan pushed the Danes northwards, and destroyed their new Danish kingdom of York.

Sometimes called 'Æthelstan the Glorious', he apparently never lost a battle. With similarities to his grandfather, he oversaw the translation of the Bible into English.

Edmund I
939 - 946

Brother to Athelstan, he recaptured areas of the North of England which had been occupied by the Vikings.

Edmund also established a period of peaceful relations with Scotland.

During his reign there was a revival of Monasticism. He came to a gruesome end being murdered in his palace by an exiled robber.

Edred

946 - 955

Another brother to Athelstan, Edred succeeded in bringing Northumbria permanently under English rule.

He continued the support of Monasticism. He was a weak man in regards to his health, and suffered from a wasting disease, which meant he often was unable to eat.

He died when he was only in his 30s with no direct heir.

Edwy
955 - 959

One of the sons of Edmund I, he became King on Edred's death, having now reached a suitable age, possibly only 15.

His reign didn't have a promising start when he had an argument with the Bishop of London, Dunstan, during his coronation. Apparently, Edwy left the coronation to visit his future bride and Dunstan went after him!

By 957 the nobles in the North were fed up of Edwy and proclaimed his brother Edgar as their king. Edwy continued as King of the south of England until his death in 959.

Edgar
959 - 975

Edgar reigned in the north from 957, but officially over England from 959. His reign was peaceful after the battles endured since Athelstan's reign. He was only 13 when he became King.

He focused on the religious revival and growth of Monasticism. This was the time of illuminated manuscripts and the building of abbeys with stained glass windows.

He worked closely with Dunstan, Bishop of London, unlike his brother Edwy. The coronation ceremony we know today originates from Edgar's coronation at Bath.

Edward
975 - 978

After the peace of Edgar's reign, England now entered a period of upheaval. Edward, Edgar's son, became King in 975 but was murdered only 3 years later at the age of 16 at Corfe Castle in Dorset.

The murderer was apparently his stepmother who had wanted her own son, Ethelred, to be king. Both boys had a legitimate claim to the throne, but Ethelred being only 6 or 7 on Egdar's death was not deemed suitable.

It was also the first of many quarrels over the next 500 years when the heir to the throne was a child and their legitimacy was also questioned. Edward has gone down in history as Edward the Martyr.

Ethelred II
978 - 1013 (16)

Nicknamed the 'Unready', Ethelred was a weak ruler who became king at the young age of 10 on the murder of his step brother Edward.

Over the next decades England was constantly invaded by the Danes. Ethelred was driven into exile in 1013 by Sweyn of Denmark and Sweyn became king of England. He died in 1014, Ethelred was invited back by the nobles, but the invasion by Canute in 1015 quickly saw his rule destroyed again.

Ethelred died in 1016 leaving his son Edmund to continue the fight with the Danes.

Edmund II
1016

Known as Edmund Ironside, his reign was short-lived. He carried on the struggle against Canute and the Danes, but was a much stronger character than his father.

In fact, he was such a good warrior that Canute agreed to share England with him.

However, Edmund mysteriously died suddenly in November 2016... was he murdered?! Leaving Canute to become King of England...

Canute
1016 - 1035

One of the most powerful men to have ever ruled England, Canute had 3 kingdoms during his time as King of England. He gained Denmark in 1019 and Norway in 1028. Having Norway gave him territory as big as an Empire, spreading all the way to Greenland.

Canute had no confidence in his descendants keeping his empire, but kept England in good order while King. As a devout Christian he continued the religious revival from Egdar's reign.

He also ensured he had no threat to his rule while King by sending 2 of Edmund Ironside's sons to Hungary, hoping they would never return. Canute died in 1035 with his Empire still intact.

Harold I

1035 - 1040

Chaos followed the strong rule of Canute. Harold (nicknamed Harefoot) was named as Regent while his brother Harthacanute was in Denmark.

In 1036 he murdered another potential rival to the throne, Alfred the Aethling, son of Ethelred II and then proclaimed himself King.

To his credit, Harold protected England from Scottish and Welsh invaders but did little else before he died in 1040.

Harthacanute
1040 - 1042

Harthacanute has gone down in History as a villain and ruffian.

He apparently dug up his brother Harold's body and threw it in a fen. He burnt down Worcester when 2 tax collectors were murdered there.

He reigned only 2 years before dying in 1042, most probably from alcohol poisoning, but left an heir to the throne after summoning another son of Ethelred II in 1041 and designating him as his heir.

Edward the Confessor
1042 - 1066

Famous for the building of Westminster Abbey, Edward was a sincerely religious and peaceful ruler. In spite of perceived weakness and focusing on religion only, Edward was actually a strong ruler and determined to keep his throne. He sent the Godwin family into exile after Earl Godwin tried to raise an army against him.

After 25 years of exile in Normandy, he had many Norman supporters who he gave important posts to which many in England didn't like. In spite of these issues England was mainly at peace during Edward's reign.

He died leaving the monarchy in chaos as in 1052 he had promised the throne to his cousin Duke William of Normandy, but later on to Harold the son of Earl Godwin when they had resolved their quarrel.

Harold II
1066

Harold was crowned King the day after Edward's death on 6th January 1066. He had been part of Edward's government, the old King's brother-in-law, and also promised the throne.

However, he was destined to be the last Anglo-Saxon monarch. William of Normandy had also been promised the throne and was not going to let that lie. Harald Hardrada of Norway also claimed to be the rightful heir of King Canute. Harold was a strong ruler and successfully killed Hardrada at the Battle of Stamford Bridge in September 1066.

He was immediately met with the invasion of William and after marching 402km south he was killed at the Battle of Hastings in October 1066. The Bayeux Tapestry portrays him being shot in the eye, or chopped down with an axe. Probably it was both!

William I
1066 - 1087

William (the Conqueror) was the first Norman King of England and the last successful invader! He was a ruthless harsh monarch who quickly stamped his authority and power on England. Anyone who questioned him was ruthlessly squashed. But those who obeyed were rewarded.

Norman barons quickly replaced English nobles. He will always be remembered for the Feudal System (which basically made the peasants slaves), Castle building and the Domesday Book.

His influence and impact had long lasting consequences on England both in the language and the landscape.

William II
1087 - 1100

William left 3 sons, Robert became Duke of Normandy, William Rufus became King and and the youngest son Henry became a thorn in William II's side and possibly his murderer. William II became known as 'Rufus' because of his angry red face!

He forced Normandy from Robert in 1096, who then went on a crusade. William II was even more harsh than his father and was very unpopular amongst the English. He used the Church only to get money, and quarrelled with Anselm the Archbishop of Canterbury over the Pope having more power than the King.

On 2nd August 1100 William Rufus was mysteriously killed by an arrow in the New Forest. His brother Henry happened to be hunting at the same time and quickly fled to Winchester and was then crowned King Henry I on 5th August. Had Henry murdered William?

Henry I
1100 - 1135

Henry's first job as King was to ensure his brother Robert was no threat to him. Robert arrived back from crusading to find Henry waiting for him in Normandy. Robert was imprisoned for the rest of his life - 28 years.

Henry was greedy, cruel and ruthless as King, but a successful ruler. He reorganised the taxation system, ensuring there was no cheating and created the King's Court meaning all fines went to him rather than pocketed by judges. Henry spent a lot of his reign fighting abroad to defend Normandy, but he left a well-organised and structured kingdom at home.

Disaster struck in 1120 when his son William was drowned in a shipwreck, leaving only a daughter Matilda. Henry made his barons swear allegiance to Matilda as his heir, but Henry died in 1135 knowing there was little chance she would become the next monarch. Monarchs needed to be warriors!

Stephen
1135 - 1154

Stephen of Blois (France) was crowned King 3 weeks after Henry's death. He was nephew to the old King, and welcomed by the barons who were not prepared to have a Queen on the throne. Matilda was not prepared to give up so easily and Stephen's reign was dominated by war with Matilda.

She had support from Scotland, and others of her family caused trouble in the West Country and Normandy. Matilda was never strong enough to beat Stephen, and he was never cruel enough to be ruthless. She succeeded as far as imprisoning Stephen in 1141 and marched to London to be crowned, but she proved unpopular with the Londoners and they went against her.

Matilda gave up in 1148 but her son Henry Plantagenet continued the fight. After the death of Stephen's son Eustace in 1153, Henry was declared heir to the throne. Stephen died in October 1154, having never recovered from Eustace's death.

Henry II
1154 - 1189

Henry II the first Plantagenet King, will always be remembered for the murder of Thomas Becket in 1170. Henry was King of quite a vast empire - Normandy, Anjou and Aquitaine along with England.

Henry restored law and order in England after the wars and upheaval of Stephen's reign but landed up in a political war with the Church over who should have jurisdiction over the priests.

Henry appointed his friend Becket as Archbishop of Canterbury hoping he would support him. However, Henry was bitterly disappointed when Becket sided with the Church, resulting in his murder by four knights in Canterbury Cathedral in 1170. Henry also had problems within his own family and died in 1189 with both his sons Richard and John at war with him.

Richard I
1189 - 1199

Known as the Lionheart, Richard became King after his father's death and has gone down in history as a mighty warrior and crusader. However, this chivalry and heroism did not come cheap and Richard almost destroyed England by selling so much land, earldoms and Church posts to raise money for the Third Crusade (1189-92).

Richard went away to war leaving England in disarray and his brother John plotting to undermine his power. Richard came home in 1194 to raise more money and then went away never to be seen in England again.

Richard died in 1199.

John
1199 - 1216

King John has gone down in history as one of the most unpopular and unsuccessful kings of England. His quarrel with the Pope meant England was exiled from the Church in 1208. He ruled like a dictator over the barons, raised endless taxes and lost wars with France and therefore almost all of Henry II's great empire.

The Barons were so fed up by 1215 that they presented John with the Magna Carta which attempted to reduce the power of the King.

The long term impact of Magna Carta is still present today in our judicial system. John died in 1216 and left his 9 year old son Henry as his heir.

Henry III
1216 - 1272

Henry was the longest serving monarch until George III. He was only 9 when his father John died so the Church and Barons set up a Regency and ruled until 1227. Once in power officially Henry immediately quarrelled with his barons as he preferred the friends of his French wife Eleanor. Henry also spent endless money on wars trying to win back the lost French lands.

By 1258 the barons had had enough and Simon de Montfort, the Earl of Leicester, drew up the Provisions of Oxford which involved the setting up of a Privy Council of 15 barons to advise the King and oversee administration.

This soon collapsed and Montfort raised a rebellion against Henry in 1264. Henry and his eldest son Edward were defeated and captured and Montfort reigned in Henry's name until 1265 when he was killed at the Battle of Evesham. For the next 7 years Henry had very little to do with government and allowed Edward to take charge and then become King Edward I on his death in 1272.

Edward I
1272 - 1307

Edward was a great warrior and a wise ruler. He worked with Parliament and from 1295 agreed not to raise taxes without Parliament's consent. His 'Model' Parliament in 1295 was the first one to contain representatives from the Church, Barons and Commons.

He wanted to rule all of Britain meaning wars with Wales and Scotland. He easily won in Wales and built castles to keep control. From 1284 Wales was brought into the English legal system. His first son Edward was born at Caernarvon Castle and became the first Prince of Wales.

He did not have the same success in Scotland and the war dominated the rest of his reign. In 1290 Edward's wife Eleanor died and her body was ceremonially carried from Lincoln to Westminster with a memorial cross erected at every one of the 12 resting places, including what became known as Charing Cross. Edward died in 1307 on his way to fight another campaign against the Scots.

Edward II
1307 - 1327

Edward II was a very different ruler from his father Edward I. He had no interest in Parliament and government or even war. Instead he devoted his time and money on the Gascon knight, Piers Gaveston and other favourites and neglected the barons and even his Queen,

Isabella of France.

His reign was dominated by rebellions from the barons and civil war. Gaveston was murdered in 1312 by the barons. Edward finally got revenge in 1321 when, with the support of Hugh Despenser and his son they got the domination of the barons. Queen Isabella however went against her husband, and joined forces in France with Roger Mortimer.

They returned to England with an army and Edward was taken prisoner, forced to renounce the throne in favour of his son Edward and murdered in Berkeley Castle - legend says with a red hot poker.

Edward III
1327 - 1377

The first 3 years of Edward's reign were dominated by Queen Isabella and Roger Mortimer. However by 1330, Edward was 18 and strong enough to seize power from them.

Edward then developed a magnificent court, excellent relations with his barons and was very successful in war. Victories at Crecy in 1346 and Poitiers in 1356 meant England won back almost one quarter of France. However, in spite of Edward's popularity and strength there were disasters during his reign.

The Black Death hit Europe in 1347, killing a third of the population. From 1364 the new king of France, Charles V, began taking back the lands Edward had gained. Then in 1376, Edward's son, the Black Prince, died followed by Edward in 1377. Once again England was left with a child King - Richard the son of the Black Prince.

Richard II
1377 - 1399

Richard was only 10 when he became King and his uncle, John of Gaunt the Duke of Lancaster, attempted to be his protector. However, Richard believed in the Divine Right of Kings and that he could do as he pleased so ignored any advice from his uncle and the barons.

Richard's reign was dominated by the 100 years war with France meaning more and more taxes were being raised by Parliament. The introduction of the Poll Tax led to the Peasants' Revolt in 1381. His quarrels with the barons also dominated his reign. In 1388 five nobles the 'Lords Appellant' had Richard's friends charged with treason and hung, drawn and quartered.

Richard took revenge 11 years later when he had 2 of the appellants arrested and the other 3 exiled including the son of John of Gaunt, Henry Bolingbroke. After Gaunt's death Richard made the mistake of seizing all Henry's lands resulting in his capture and deposition. He was murdered in Pontefract Castle in 1400, Henry having become King Henry IV in 1399.

Henry IV
1399 - 1413

The first Lancastrian King, Henry's reign was overshadowed by the fact that he was a usurper to the throne. Even though Richard had been unpopular he was the rightful King, whereas Henry was the grandson of Edward III by his 3rd son. There were plenty of other descendants of Edward III who had better claims.

There were many rebellions against him even by barons who had been his supporters. In 1403 Henry became ill with paralysis which many saw as a punishment. Battles with France, Wales and Scotland also dominated his reign, meaning more taxes needing to be raised from Parliament.

By the end of his reign there were constant fighting factions within the court and Henry increasingly incapacitated. He died in 1413.

Henry V
1413 - 1422

Seen as a temporary 'blip' in the nobility quarrels which caused the Wars of the Roses, Henry V was a magnificent warrior King very different from his father. His huge successes in the wars against France, in particular the huge victory at Agincourt in 1415, saw Henry being recognised as the heir to the French King, Charles VI.

This was further cemented when Henry married Charles' daughter Catherine in 1420. Tragically none of this was to last and Henry died from dysentery, caused from so much battlefield fighting, in 1422.

He left as his heir, his baby son, Henry VI. And the start of the Wars of the Roses...

Henry VI
1422 - 1461 and 1470 - 1471

With a child king on the throne, the Yorkist descendants of Richard II were determined to seize their chance to claim their right to the throne. All began relatively smoothly with Henry VI's uncles ruling for him, but they soon became unpopular when they started losing France in 1429 with the rise of Joan of Arc. By 1453, all of France was lost, Henry VI was ruling in his own right but had also begun to go insane. He had been a weak ruler, with a very dominant Queen Margaret. With his first bout of insanity Richard Duke of York seized his chance and went to war with Henry and his Lancastrian lords. The first battle at St Albans in 1455 was a disaster for Henry and he was taken prisoner, however Queen Margaret was not to be defeated and she won against the Yorkists in 1460, killing the Duke of York.

However, by 1461, Henry and his army were defeated again, put in the Tower of London and Edward Duke of York became Edward IV. Henry did have one more chance of being King when 9 years later he regained the throne but immediately lost it in 1471. The Battle of Tewkesbury also saw the death of Henry's son and heir followed by the alleged murder of Henry VI at the Tower.

Edward IV
1461 - 1470 and 1471 - 1483

Edward was the son of Richard Duke of York killed at Wakefield in 1460. He was a strong and determined King very different from Henry VI. He chose his own wife Elizabeth Woodville possibly for love rather than marrying the French Princess chosen for him.

The first 9 years of his reign were overshadowed by the Lancastrian threat and quarrels with his cousin the Earl of Warwick. Warwick eventually defected to the Lancastrian side and was a key player in the battles of 1470.

It seems Warwick and other nobles were most put out by his marriage choice. However from 1471 with the defeat of the Lancastrians, the death of Warwick, and the end of the civil wars, trade revived and the monarchy became rich and powerful.

He reigned unchallenged until his death in 1483.

Edward V
1483

Edward IV left as his heir his 12 year old son Edward. Once again a child King and the beginning of another tempestuous few years for the monarchy. Edward was crowned King Edward V with his uncle Richard Duke of Gloucester given the job of Protector.

However, what then happened is still subject to great debate and mystery. In July 1483, Richard deposed his nephew, was crowned Richard III and Edward V and his brother were put in the Tower of London and after August never seen again.

Did Richard murder them? Did Henry Tudor the new Lancastrian leader have them killed? This will remain as one of the most mysterious plots in history.

Richard III
1483 - 1485

With such a dubious ascent to the throne Richard III did not stand much chance of success. He supported his claim by declaring the Princes in the Tower illegitimate. But there was too much suspicion surrounding him and he had a lot of enemies amongst the nobility.

He was met with a rebellion led by the Duke of Buckingham in October 1483 which he overthrew but it showed how little support Richard had. As King he worked hard to be a just ruler, operating the courts fairly and respecting the Church. But this was not enough and when his only son died in 1484 his position was very weak.

By 1485, the Lancastrians had raised an army under Henry Tudor and fought Richard III at the Battle of Bosworth in August. Richard III fought to the bitter end and was killed. The story goes that his crown was found hanging from a thornbush and given to Henry Tudor, shortly afterwards crowned Henry VII.

Henry VII
1485 - 1509

 The first King of the Tudor Dynasty and the man who finally ended the Wars of the Roses, Henry VII was a shrewd and determined ruler. Henry married Elizabeth of York, the daughter of Edward IV, finally joining the warring families together.

His reign was not without its challenges however, with threats from two Pretenders to the throne - Lambert Simnel in 1487 and Perkin Warbeck in the 1490s. Simnel's rebellion led to the Battle of Stoke, seen as the final battle of the Wars of the Roses but Henry VII had no difficulty in defeating the few remaining Yorkist rebels.

Warbeck's was more challenging involving war with France but Warbeck was finally defeated and killed in 1499. After that Henry reigned peacefully and built up a very efficient administration ensuring the Crown became financially secure. He avoided war, using diplomacy when possible and when he died in 1509, left a stable and wealthy crown.

Henry VIII
1509 - 1547

Henry was not born to be king. He was the 2nd son of Henry VII, and only became heir to the throne on the death of his elder brother Arthur in 1501. When his father died in 1509, Henry was a handsome young 18 year old, who married his late brother's wife Catherine of Aragon. In his early years, Henry focused on hunting and wars with France and Scotland. He aspired to be a warrior King and was determined to reclaim the French crown.

However by the 1520s he became increasingly worried by his lack of a son. His request for an annulment was nothing unusual for Kings at that time but the Pope had recently made an alliance with Emperor Charles V who was nephew to Catherine of Aragon, and therefore did not give the answer Henry wanted. Thus followed the Break with Rome in 1534, his divorce from Catherine and his marriage to Anne Boleyn. However, Anne also failed to produce a son, and it was not until his marriage to Jane Seymour in 1536 that a son was finally born in 1537. The rest of Henry's reign was taken up with political warring between the Catholic and Protestant factions at Court, 3 more wives and a renewal of wars with France and Scotland. By the 1540s, Henry suffered badly with gout and died in 1547, leaving his 6th wife Catherine Parr and his 3 children, Mary, Elizabeth and Edward.

Edward VI
1547 - 1553

Edward came to the throne at the age of 9 and amazingly as a child King he reigned unchallenged. He was the son of Henry's 3rd wife Jane Seymour and was brought up as a Protestant with his sister Elizabeth.

The Duke of Somerset was chosen as Lord Protector and helped Edward rule successfully until the rebellions of 1549 saw him overthrown by the Duke of Northumberland who took over the Protectorship.

During Edward's reign the Protestant Reformation took hold, with further Dissolution of the Monasteries, the publication of the Book of Common Prayer, and the simplifying of the Churches. A popular King, Edward VI suffered with ill health and died of TB in 1553 at the age of 16.

Lady Jane Grey

1553

The Nine Days Queen, Lady Jane Grey was crowned Queen on the death of Edward VI. A distant cousin of Edward VI, 15 year old Jane was declared Edward's heir because she was a devout Protestant who would further the Reformation in England.

However, Henry VIII's Will, approved by Act of Parliament, had said that Mary, the daughter of Catherine of Aragon, would be the next Monarch if Edward died with no children.

Once Jane was crowned, the supporters of Mary raised a rebellion and 9 days later Jane was overthrown and Mary crowned. Lady Jane Grey was executed a few months later which horrified many in England and her story is one of the saddest in the history of the monarchy.

Mary I
1553 - 1558

Forever known as 'Bloody Mary', the eldest child of Henry VIII by his first marriage had an unhappy few years as Queen. Brought up a strict Roman Catholic and a witness to her mother's divorce, Mary was determined to make England Catholic again so overturned the Reformation of Edward's reign.

As the rightful heir to Edward, many in England were initially supportive of the new Queen. However, her marriage to Prince Philip of Spain, later King of Spain, and her disastrous foreign policy resulting in the loss of Calais meant her popularity rapidly declined. Her strict laws against Protestants saw many go into exile onto the Continent, while hundreds of others lost their lives at the stake - the Martyrs. Archbishop Thomas Cranmer who had been so influential under Henry VIII and Edward VI was one of the most high profile martyrs.

Mary's personal life was also beset with sadness as she failed to produce an heir and with her husband often out of the country this became increasingly impossible. By 1558 Mary was ill and she died in November having agreed to pass the crown to her half sister Elizabeth in the hope that England would remain Catholic.

Elizabeth I

1558 - 1603

The 'Virgin Queen' has become almost a legendary figure in how she has been portrayed in history. The daughter of Anne Boleyn, Henry VIII's second wife, Elizabeth was brought up with her young brother Edward as a Protestant and was welcomed with relief and hope as Queen in 1558. Her long reign is famous for successes in religious,foreign and domestic policies. Elizabeth's religious settlement created the Church of England - a mix of Protestant doctrine and Catholic elements in the look of the Church.

The victory against the Spanish Armada in 1588 has gone down as one of England's finest moments, and the likes of Sir Francis Drake saw England beginning the exploration and settlement of the New World. Elizabeth's introduction of the Poor Laws saw the beginnings of a very basic welfare state with the founding of hospitals and almshouses.

Elizabeth also faced many rebellions resulting in the execution of her cousin Mary Queen of Scots. There was still no religious liberty outside the Church of England with persecution of Catholics and Puritans. Elizabeth refused to marry and so died in 1603 with no direct heir and thus the end of the Tudor dynasty.

James I
1603 - 1625

Elizabeth chose as her heir the son of Mary Queen of Scots. James had been King James VI of Scotland since the execution of his mother and now for the first time united the Crowns of England and Scotland together as King James I of England.

James is infamous as being the King planned to be blown up on 5th November by the Catholic Guy Fawkes and his fellow conspirators. James also oversaw the final thorough translation of the Bible into English - the Authorised, King James Version. Religious intolerance against Puritans as well as Catholics, saw the Pilgrim Fathers flee to America in 1620.

James was popular in Scotland and had a fairly equal relationship with the Scottish nobility. However, he failed to understand how politics worked in England and did not respect Parliament, particularly in regards to taxation. As a result he began to rule absolutely and thus became increasingly unpopular. He died in 1625 leaving political and financial instability.

Charles I
1625 - 1649

The only king to be put on trial and executed, Charles I had a tumultuous reign. Charles believed in the Divine Right of Kings and from 1629 ruled without Parliament - the Personal Rule- until 1640 when he was obliged to call them back as he needed money.

Parliament had other reasons to distrust Charles, his wife was openly Roman Catholic and he himself promoted Catholic elements within the Church of England. By 1642 relations between the King and Parliament completely broke down when Charles attempted to arrest the five MPs who were his biggest critics. Both sides raised an army and the Battle of Edgehill began a six year Civil War between Parliament and the Royalists. By 1648 Charles had run out of money, while Parliament under the leadership of Oliver Cromwell had developed a highly disciplined New Model Army who easily started defeating the Royalist Army from 1645.

In January 1649 Charles was defeated, captured and put on trial and found guilty of 'traitorously and maliciously levying war against the present Parliament and the people therein represented'. On 30th January 1649 Charles I was executed outside Banqueting House in Whitehall and the monarchy was abolished.

Oliver Cromwell
1649 - 1658(60)

Technically not a monarch, Oliver Cromwell 'ruled' over England after the execution of Charles I. Scotland refused to acknowledge Cromwell as ruler and actually crowned Charles' son Charles II.

However, Charles became a fugitive from 1651 after his failed attempt to invade England. From 1653 Cromwell was given the title 'Lord Protector' and actually offered the title King in 1657 but he refused. A devout Puritan, Cromwell encouraged sobriety in all areas of life and Sundays were made by law to be a day of rest. Religious liberty was allowed to all Protestants and Jews were welcomed.

However, there was no toleration of Catholics and the massacre at Drogheda in Ireland testified to this. Cromwell was a skillful politician who ruled with the help of Major-Generals who governed 11 areas of England. Cromwell's unexpected death in September 1658 left his son Richard being given the Lord Protector role, but his weak leadership saw Scotland quickly welcome Charles II back, shortly followed by England in 1660.

Charles II
1660 - 1685

The 'Merry Monarch' ruled through what became known as the 'Restoration' period where England and Scotland became a Monarchy again. Charles was welcomed by many as the legitimate ruler.

His first decade as monarch was overshadowed by the Great Plague in 1665 followed by the Fire of London in 1666. Charles took great interest in the latest science and medical discoveries with the founding of the Royal Society. Catholic and Protestant disagreements continued within Parliament and the country as a whole. Charles' marriage produced no heir but he had many illegitimate children by his several mistresses.

He made 'underhand' deals with France by his dubious foreign policy and there was political instability throughout his reign. From 1681 he ruled as an absolute King showing similarity to his father Charles I. In spite of this, Charles managed to survive as King but with no legitimate heir his death in 1685 left the country in disarray yet again.

James II
1685 - 1688

James was the younger brother of Charles II. He openly declared himself as a Roman Catholic and made it clear that he did not want to rule with Parliament.

From 1686 it was clear that James was intent on aiming to reintroduce Roman Catholicism as the official religion of the country. Parliament which initially had many royalist supporters, began to lose trust in James and they were permanently dismissed in 1687. When the Queen gave birth to a son in June 1688, the fears that Catholicism would become permanent intensified.

Parliament and the Bishops decided to ask the Protestant William of Orange in Holland to invade England and take the throne for himself. As the husband of James' daughter Mary, and grandson to Charles I, William had a legitimate claim to the throne. By December 1688, James had fled to France and abdicated the crown. However, James did make one more attempt to regain the throne. In March 1690 he landed in Ireland with French troops but was defeated heavily at the Battle of the Boyne in July 1690. He went into permanent exile in France until his death in 1701.

Mary II 1660 - 1685
and
William III 1689 - 1702

The first and only time Britain has had a dual Monarchy. William and Mary were welcomed to the throne on the deposition of James II.

Forever known as the Glorious Revolution, the Parliament called in January 1689 passed the laws which was the beginning of our Constitutional Monarchy as we know it today. The Monarch was no longer allowed to be Catholic or married to one.

Parliament was also given greater power so that no Monarch could rule alone again. The Toleration Act of May 1689 saw freedom of worship granted to all except Catholics and Unitarians. The Bank of England was founded in 1694 to control public expenditure. Mary died of small-pox leaving no children in 1694. William continued ruling alone, and in 1701 the Act of Settlement ensured the Hanoverian and Protestant succession to the throne. William died in a riding accident in 1702 leaving as his heir, Anne the Protestant sister of Mary II.

Anne
1702 - 1714

A shy, stubborn Queen, Anne's reign is notable for the Act of Union with Scotland in 1707 which joined the nations politically for the first time. Great Britain was now the name most commonly used to describe England, Wales and Scotland. St Paul's Cathedral was completed by Sir Christopher Wren in 1710. Anne's reign saw the rise of political parties with the increasing power of Parliament.

Throughout her reign there was constant rivalry between the Whigs and the Tories, each trying to have the most influence over the Queen. One of the families who had the greatest influence over Anne was the Churchills - created Duke of Marlborough by William III. Marlborough was successful in leading a series of victories against the French during Anne's reign. Anne's marriage to Prince George of Denmark resulted in 17 pregnancies but only one survived to the age of 11. As a result the succession was a subject of great debate during the last years of Anne's reign, with the Whigs fully behind the Protestant Act of Settlement while the Tories were more influenced by the Stuart descendants of James II. However on the death of Anne in 1714, both parties had united in agreeing to abide by the Act of Settlement and welcomed the House of Hanover.

George I
1714 - 1727

The first Hanoverian Monarch, and unable to speak English, George I spoke to his ministers in French. In spite of his widespread unpopularity due to rumours of how he treated his wife and the greed of his German mistresses, he did try to fulfill his role properly.

He successfully saw off Jacobite rebellions which were still trying to bring the Stuarts back to the throne. George was also successful in his foreign policy, creating an alliance with France in 1717-18. His reign saw the beginnings of the role of 'Prime Minister' under the influence of Robert Walpole.

By 1724 due to scandals regarding the King's role in the South Sea Company, George relied more and more on Walpole's judgments in government. He died of a stroke in 1727 leaving his son George and a daughter Sophia who married Frederick William I of Russia.

George II
1727 - 1760

Robert Walpole continued being the chief adviser to George II, and achieved in bringing the Tories into supporting George's legitimacy as Monarch. By 1742 an increasingly popular faction led by George's son Frederick forced Walpole to resign.

George and his new adviser Earl Granville became increasingly unpopular when they brought England into the War of the Austrian Succession. Their opponents could easily claim that George was prioritising German needs over England's. Parliament forced the resignation of Granville in 1744 and William Pitt took his place 15 months later. George II was the last British King to appear on the battlefield when fighting the French in 1743, but in the last few years of his reign took little interest in politics.

Pitt oversaw Britain's strategies in the Seven Years War against France (1756-1763) while George was merely an observer. George was passionate about music and was a patron of the composer Handel. George died suddenly in 1760 leaving his grandson as heir to the throne.

George III
1760 - 1820

George III's reign was the longest until Victoria's a century later. A late developer academically and faced with huge challenges, George's reign was a time of radical change both domestically and abroad. His marriage to Queen Charlotte was a 50 year success and family was hugely important to George III.

The first decade of his reign was marked by political instability, with the king's inexperience obvious and the growth of party politics as we know today. Lord North as the Prime Minister from 1770 brought stability and calm to the Commons meaning focus could turn to the problems in the American Colonies leading to the War of Independence in 1775. Further political quarrels later on were squashed when the growth of patriotism helped support the wars against Revolutionary France in 1793.

The later years of his reign saw the onset of George's intermittent insanity causing his son to act as Regent. A popular monarch and viewed with much compassion, George's death in 1820 came amidst controversy over Catholic Emancipation.

George IV
1820 - 1830

An unpopular King, George IV had acted as Regent for his father during the last years of his reign. His marriage to Caroline of Brunswick was a disaster, resulting in one daughter, Charlotte, who died in 1817, and he was aiming for divorce when Caroline died in 1821.

His relationships with Parliament and his ministers were poor, and by 1827 he had little weight with either the Whigs or Tories. A huge change in his reign was the Catholic Emancipation Act in 1829. Interestingly, he was the first King to visit Scotland since Charles II and he also visited Ireland and Hanover.

George spent money freely building the Royal Pavillion in Brighton, and transforming Windsor Castle and Buckingham Palace. This lavish spending did not help his popularity however and he spent the last 3 years of his life alone at Windsor. He died in 1830 childless and so the throne went to his younger brother.

William IV
1830 - 1837

The 3rd son of George III, William never expected to be King, particularly at the age of 65. His early life saw him join the Royal Navy and he became the Duke of Clarence in 1789. With the death of George III's second son, he became heir to George IV.

Initially he was popular as he demonstrated none of the lavish lifestyle of George IV, preferring a simple coronation. His reign was short and dominated by the Reform Bill. William supported the Duke of Wellington's Tory government but when they lost the election soon after he became King, he was left with the challenge of a Whig government led by Lord Grey who were determined to push through the Electoral Reform Bill. 1831-32 saw many riots across the country after the Lords repeatedly refused to pass the bill.

By 1832 the King had agreed to create more Whig peers in the Lords, but this was unnecessary as the Lords did back down and pass the Reform Bill by the end of 1832. The Reform Bill extended the vote to the middle classes for the first time. The impact of the Industrial Revolution was demonstrated with new industrial towns given representation too. William died with no legitimate children in 1837, leaving the throne to his niece Victoria.

Victoria
1837 - 1901

One of the most popular and iconic Monarchs in British history, Victoria became Queen soon after her 18th birthday and saw huge changes both in Britain and the world during her long reign. Her marriage to Prince Albert produced 9 children and his death in 1861 came as a huge shock to Victoria, she famously wore black for the rest of her life. Albert worked alongside Victoria in helping increase Britain's standing in the world with the development of the British Empire. The Great Exhibition at the Crystal Palace in Hyde Park in 1851 was a huge milestone in Britain's influence and was a showcase of industry.

Victoria became the Empress of India in 1877 and developed a fascination for Indian culture and language. At home, Victoria's reign oversaw some improvement in conditions for the poor, particularly with working conditions and increasing opportunities in education for children. Victoria worked with many different Prime Ministers, including Benjamin Disraeli and William Gladstone. Her reign saw the increasingly ceremonial role of the Monarchy as Parliament became more representative and involved in government. By her death in 1901, there had been massive developments in medicine, industry and technology but also the beginnings of unrest between the European powers.

Edward VII
1901 - 1910

The longest 'heir apparent' until Prince Charles today, Edward waited 59 years to be King. While waiting he indulged in high society and Victoria had many worries about his future as Monarch. However, he proved to be more sensible as King than feared. He was a popular monarch and travelled widely in Europe developing the Triple Alliance with Russia and France. After the Boer War (1899-1902) he focused on reforming the Military by insisting on an army medical service and building up the fleet of Dreadnought battleships. His love of high society while waiting to be king, became apparent with the Edwardian period being a heyday for the upper classes.

The Edwardian period also saw the growth of the motor car and more leisure time for the middle and upper classes. These early years of the 20th century also saw more social mobility. By his death in 1910, Parliament was at gridlock over the so-called 'People's Budget' created by the Liberal government of Harold Asquith. This legislation would have brought in greater taxation of the wealthy and radical social welfare reforms. The Conservative House of Lords refused to pass the bill and when Asquith asked the King to get involved he declined, insisting it needed to be decided by the people in a General Election. Edward died in May 1910 leaving his wife, Queen Alexandra and 5 children.

George V
1910 - 1936

George V, the second son of Edward VII inherited a kingdom still enjoying the prosperity of the Edwardian period. His first task as King was to take on the political gridlock in Parliament inherited from his father.

Electoral success for the Liberals in 1911 led to the passing of the Parliament Act and the end of this crisis. The building of the Titanic was an example of a more cosmopolitan society with ambitions of world travel and more leisure. The tragic sinking of the Titanic in 1912 however, showed up the huge inequalities still present in society and the onset of the First World War two years later brought the Edwardian heyday to an end.

The First World War increased George V's popularity as he personally visited the Frontline many times. The post-war years were beset with difficulties with political crises and industrial unrest. The first Labour government was formed during his reign in 1924 and the financial crisis of 1931 saw the first National Coalition government on George's recommendation. The Silver Jubilee celebrations of 1935 demonstrated how popular George V was as King. A serious illness in 1928 saw the King having to be very careful of his health for the rest of his life. He died in January 1936 leaving a constitutional crisis.

Edward VIII
1936

Famous for his abdication due to his desire to marry Wallis Simpson, a divorcee, Edward's reign was short-lived. From the outset of becoming King he was under pressure to end his relationship with Mrs Simpson, and by December it was clear to all in the government and Royal household that he couldn't be King and also marry.

Once the press caught hold of it on 3rd December, Edward was left with little choice but to abdicate which he did on 10th December: "I, Edward the Eighth,...do hereby declare... My irrevocable determination to renounce the throne for Myself and My descendants". Once abdicated he was given the title Duke of Windsor and married Wallis Simpson in June 1937. They settled in Europe and courted controversy when he was entertained by Adolf Hitler in October 1937.

He spent the duration of the Second World War in the West Indies, coming back to live in Paris after 1945. He never had any proper reconciliation with the Royal family until he was welcomed back in 1967 to attend an unveiling of a plaque to his mother Queen Mary. Edward died in 1972 and was buried at Frogmore House in Windsor.

George VI
1936 - 1952

Never expecting to be King, George VI was the second son of George V and became King the day after the abdication of his elder brother Edward VIII. A shy and reserved character, George nevertheless rose to the challenge and became a popular and well-respected King.

Despite his speech impediment he demonstrated amazing determination to overcome this as King. He was instrumental in re-affirming an alliance with France and the USA in the lead up to the Second World War. Initially unsure of Churchill becoming Prime Minister, he became a firm supporter of Churchill throughout the war. King George and Queen Elizabeth remained in London throughout the War showing solidarity with the Londoners during the Blitz and other bombing raids. George was also a key figure behind the National Days of Prayer throughout the War. The changing role of Britain in the world after 1945 with the decline of her Empire, saw George VI become the first Head of the Commonwealth in 1949. George VI also oversaw as King the creation of the Welfare State in the Post-War years. From 1948 the King's health declined with the onset of lung cancer and his death in 1952 was much mourned throughout Britain.

Elizabeth II
1952 -

As the longest reigning Monarch, Elizabeth II has seen huge social, political, global and technological changes during her reign. Elizabeth has worked with 14 Prime Ministers, seen the break-up of the Empire and the development of the Commonwealth, and witnessed the creation of the European Union and now Britain's exit. Each decade has brought it's different challenges and ideas: the liberalisation of traditional values in the 1960s, the industrial unrest of the 1970 and 1980s, Britain's first female Prime Minister, and personal family crises and tragedy in the 1990s. There is also an increasing threat of the break-up of the United Kingdom with the rise of nationalism particularly in Scotland. Elizabeth is a popular Monarch but there are louder calls for a republic amongst many people. Globally the world has become smaller with the massive increase in air-travel and the internet. Her marriage to Prince Philip the Duke of Edinburgh has lasted over 70 years and survived the crises amongst their 4 children.

At the great age of 94 the Queen has been greeted with an unforeseen crisis in Covid-19. This, along with Brexit, potential Scottish independence and constant developments in the online world, Queen Elizabeth II has undoubtedly still got many challenges to face in her final years.

Also available from the same authors:

The Great history of Britain

by

Anne & Paul Fryer

An introduction to some of the key events in British history aimed specifically at children.

Beginning at the time of Jesus Christ and ending with an overview of Modern Britain, this book endeavours to show how events and people over the centuries are all linked together. Anyone reading this book should finish with a clear and concise overview of the chronology of 'The Great history of Britain'.

www.greathistoryofbritain.co.uk